SAN DIEGO
impressions

Mark and Kellie —
Thanks for your Car!
Bill Wechter

photography by Bill Wechter

FARCOUNTRY
PRESS

Front cover: Downtown San Diego
from the Coronado bridge.

Right: Cardiff sunset.

Previous page: Birds soar over the rocky
shoreline of La Jolla Cove.

Back cover: Oceanside Municipal Pier.

ISBN 1-56037-275-3
Photographs © 2004 by Bill Wechter
© 2004 Farcountry Press

For more information on our books write
Farcountry Press, P.O. Box 5630, Helena, MT 59604,
call (800) 821-3874, or visit www.farcountrypress.com.

Created, produced, and designed in the United States.
Printed in China.

Facing page: Sailing in San Diego Bay.

Below: Cabrillo National Monument, on Pt. Loma.

With the self-proclaimed slogan "America's Finest City," one would think there is something special about San Diego. Well, there is.

Start with the balmy climate—predominately blue skies and temperatures that brush the 70s in the dead of winter, clothing residents in shorts, T-shirts, and sandals for a better portion of the year and arousing the envy of many across the rest of the nation.

San Diego's active, vibrant lifestyle can leave you breathless. Swimming, surfing, hiking, running, sailing, scuba diving, biking, and hang gliding are commonplace. For the more devoted, triathlons and marathons can be found.

All this in a glimmering city on a bay at the edge of the Pacific Ocean, with beaches and palm trees galore and a backcountry of forested mountains that descend eastward to a pristine desert habitat.

Add San Diego's rich history—from Native Americans, to the explorer Juan Rodríguez Cabrillo in 1542 and more than 200 years of Spanish settlement, including the earliest of a series of Catholic missions that eventually stretched from Baja California to San Francisco, to the incorporation of San Diego as an American city in 1850 and the birth of naval aviation at North Island in 1917. Then add the international border with Tijuana, Mexico, the busiest border crossing in the country. And then the revitalized urban core with restaurants and night clubs, a convention center, and a new professional baseball stadium…and one starts to get the feel for San Diego.

From Balboa Park to the Oceanside Pier, from Tijuana to the Gaslamp Quarter, from Cabrillo National Monument to the Anza Borrego Desert State Park, I have strived to capture on film the character of San Diego and to celebrate it on the pages of this book.

Bill Wechter

Right: Saluting naval officer.

Below: Marine recruits at Camp Pendleton during the final leg of the "Crucible," a 54-hour training exercise—one of the last before they become Marines.

Facing page: The Blue Angels perform at the Miramar Air Show.

Right: U.S. Coast Guard lighthouse on the western tip of Point Loma.

Far right: The San Diego Convention Center opened in 1989 and welcomed its four millionth out-of-state visitor in 2003.

Right: San Diego on the move. Downtown continues to rise high behind the *Star of India,* considered the world's oldest active sailing ship.

Below: Horse-drawn carriage and the Hyatt Hotel, downtown San Diego.

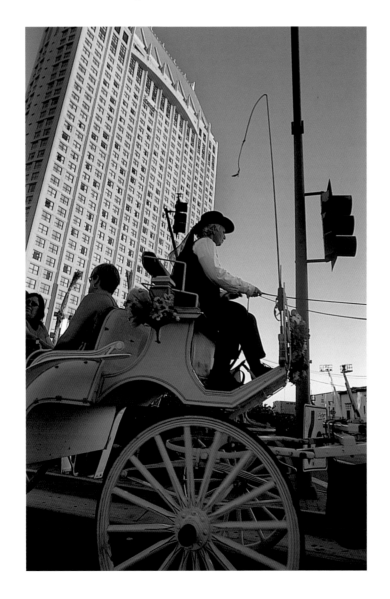

Facing page: The San Diego–Coronado Bridge, seen here from Seaport Village, connects downtown with Coronado Island.

Below: At a slower pace, visitors can also travel between the city and Coronado by ferry.

Old Town San Diego State Historic Park, "the Birthplace of California."

Historic homes in Heritage Park in Old Town San Diego State Historic Park,
with a modern home rising high in the background.

Facing page: Old Town's Casa de Estudillo, residence of the first Mexican administrators of the city, now displays furnishings of the Mexican California era.

Left: Bazaar del Mundo mural, Old Town.

Below: The Bazaar del Mundo is a continuous festival of food, markets, and music.

17

Facing page: Courtyard of Mission Basilica San Diego de Alcala.

Left: Replica of bells that marked El Camino Real, the road that connected the Spanish missions along the California coast.

Below: Mission Basilica San Diego de Alcala, founded in 1769 by Junipero Serra, is a National and State Historic Landmark.

Following pages: Summer's playground: Pacific Beach from Crystal Pier.

Facing page: The Giant Dipper, built in 1925, Belmont Park, Mission Beach.

Right: Cruising the boardwalk, Mission Beach to Pacific Beach.

Below: Ice cream, hot dogs, and a whole lot more—Pacific Beach.

Right: The lily pond is always a serene approach to the 1915 Botanical Building, at Balboa Park.

Below: California poppies, the State flower.

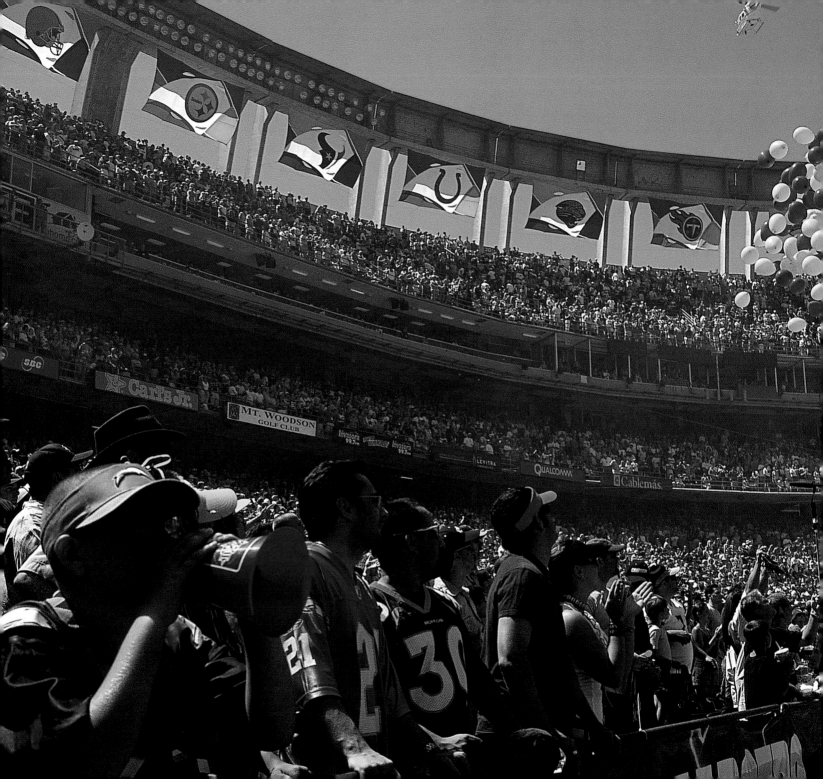

Left: Sunday in the stadium with 65,000 Charger fans.

Below top: San Diego State University Aztec cheerleaders.

Below bottom: San Diego Chargers quarterback Drew Brees alludes Denver Bronco Trevor Pryce.

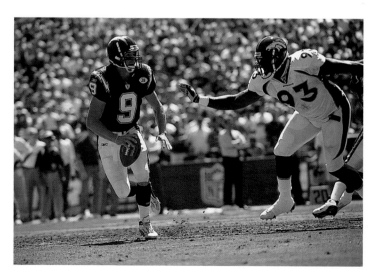

Above: Parasailers at Torrey Pines Gliderport. The history
of gliding and soaring here goes back to the 1920s.

Right: Low tide and sunset at Solana Beach.

Facing page: Nesting egrets in San Elijo Lagoon.

Left: Blue heron.

Below: San Elijo Lagoon, nesting grounds for sixty-five bird species.

Above: San Diego skyline at dusk, from Coronado Island.

Facing page: Palomar Observatory, in North San Diego County, houses the famous 200-inch Hale Telescope. The brightest light to the left of the telescope is the planet Mars during its closest approach to earth in 60,000 years.

Following pages: Kelp forest tank at Birch Aquarium, Scripps Institution of Oceanography.

Above: City Ballet of San Diego performs a summer afternoon show at the Organ Pavilion, Balboa Park.

Left: Spanish Colonial architecture in Balboa Park, built to host the Panama–California Exposition of 1915.

San

Above: Bea Evenson Fountain on the Plaza de Balboa,
and the House of Hospitality, Balboa Park.

Facing page: A glimpse of El Prado walkway, Balboa Park.

Right: Swami's Beach sunset. Red sky at night, sailor's delight.

Below: Spanish shawl nudibranch in a Cardiff tidepool.

Above: An Encinitas welcome, and Woodies at La Paloma Theater, built in 1927.

Left: Moving fast into Cardiff on Coast Highway 101.

Left: Ripping the crystal blue at Swami's.

Below: Entrance to Swami's Beach, Encinitas,
a world-famous surf spot.

Left: Hippopotamus don't miss a thing at the San Diego Zoo, Balboa Park.

Below: Flamingos greet visitors at the San Diego Zoo entrance.

Below and right: Sea anemone and seastar, Cardiff tidepool.

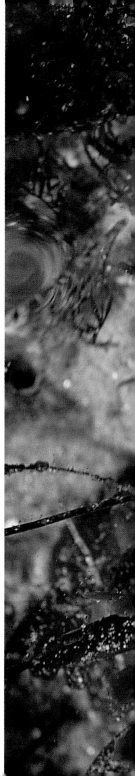

Left: USS *Constellation,* Kitty Hawk class aircraft carrier and "America's Flagship."

Below: Sailors at Naval Station North Island, and a Harrier jet landing at sea.

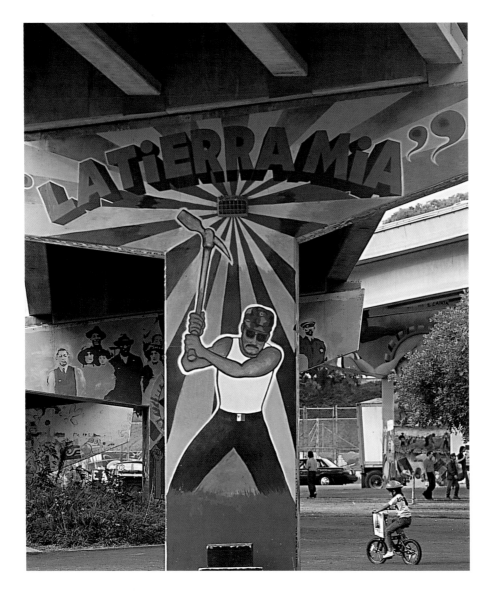

Above: Chicano Park, Logan Heights, under the Coronado Bridge.

Right: The San Diego County Fair always packs the Del Mar Fairgrounds.

Following pages: The Hotel Del Coronado, built in 1888, is a National Historic Landmark.

Left: Wind-gnarled Torrey pines at Torrey Pines State Reserve. This rare tree species is found only in this small preserve south of Del Mar and on an island off Santa Barbara, 200 miles away.

Below: Teddy bear cholla cactus, Anza-Borrego Desert.

Left: Crystal Pier Hotel, Pacific Beach, but who wants to stay in a hotel room?

Below: Bodyboarders on the Oceanside Pier.

Right: The town of Julian in the Cuyamaca Mountains brings
San Diegans for apple pies and fresh mountain air.

Below: Dock on Lake Cuyamaca, south of Julian.

Above: 'Giant Tecolote' ranunculus in bloom from early March through early May at the famous Carlsbad flower fields.

Facing page: The Encinitas flower farms are big agribusiness in North San Diego County.

Above: The paddock affords a close look at the competitors on their way to the track.

Left: Down the home stretch at the Del Mar racetrack, "Where the Surf Meets the Turf."

Above: Rocks balanced: a public "sculpture" for all to enjoy in Cardiff.

Facing page: Lightning put on a remarkable show, but to an empty house here in Oceanside.

Above: Sunset from atop Mount Soledad, the highest point in
the city of San Diego and a traditional Easter gathering place.

Left: The Salk Institute for Biological Studies in La Jolla,
designed by architect Louis I. Kahn.

Left: Saint James by the Sea Episcopal Church in La Jolla, and the La Jolla Contempory Museum of Art bronze sculpture "ghandiG" by Peter Shelton.

Below: Sacred Heart Church of Ocean Beach sees many a jet depart San Diego International Airport.

Left: Contemporary Southern California living: a condominium in downtown San Diego.

Below: Glass design by Joan Irving at the San Diego International Airport.

Three playful dolphins bodysurf at Torrey Pines State Beach.

Facing page: Auto entrance to Mexico from the San Ysidro border crossing pedestrian bridge.

Left: Street vendor with bargains, at the Otay Mesa international border crossing.

Above: Winter fun on Palomar Mountain, northeast
San Diego County.

Right: Frost nips the grasses and trees on the way up
Palomar Mountain.

Right: A flying orca impresses the crowd at SeaWorld San Diego, on Mission Bay.

Below: Everyone seems to want to pet the bottlenose dolphins at SeaWorld.

Right: San Diego Gaslamp Quarter, downtown.

Below: Old house downtown on Date Street near Little Italy.

Left: Pleasure sailing, commerical shipping, and the U.S. Navy, all on San Diego Bay.

Below: Sailing on Mission Bay.

Left: Mountain meadow in Cuyamaca Rancho State Park.

Below: Southern mule deer buck near Lake Cuyamaca.

Above: Mariachi band entertains in a La Jolla park.

Facing page: Two main drags: El Cajon Boulevard and Park Boulevard.

Facing page: Two hours' drive from San Diego is the 600,000-acre Anza-Borrego Desert State Park.

Below: Barrel cactus flower, Anza-Borrego Desert.

Left: Cutting a wave in Oceanside.

Following pages: Sunset at the Oceanside Municipal Pier.

'57 Chevy Bel Air, with accessories.

Wind 'n Sea beach, La Jolla.

*B*ill Wechter rarely leaves his camera at home. For Bill, taking photographs is a lifestyle and a passion. One can see it in his work.

> *Pictures happen all the time and at all times of the day. You are bound by those circumstances. You can't make photographs happen when you want them. You've gotta make them when they happen.*

Bill has been a photojournalist for more than twenty years and is currently a staff photographer for the *North County Times*. Over the past few years his personal photography has grown and diversified. As a 1982 graduate of the University of New Mexico, he was drawn to the open landscape of the Southwest, and his work reflected its mysterious vastness. More recently Bill has enjoyed photographing the magnificent San Diego coastline and local wildlife. He has also traveled to Hawaii, Cuba, Haiti, New York City, Baja California, and the High Sierras, where he has captured the essence of the cultural and natural environments. His work has been exhibited in galleries in San Diego and New York City.

Bill Wechter gradually moved to the West Coast from his hometown of Northport, New York, and currently resides in Solana Beach, California, with his wife Michèle.

www.billwechterphotos.com.